Kaleido-scopes

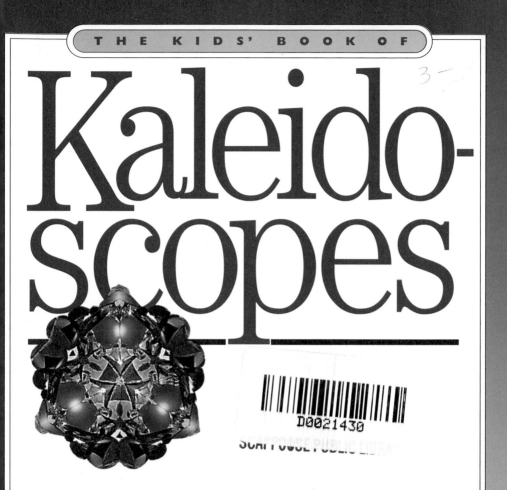

By Carolyn Bennett
With Jack Romig

Photography by John Bean
Illustrations by David Cain

WORKMAN PUBLISHING • NEW YORK

Library of Congress Cataloging-in-Publication Data
Bennett, Carolyn.
The kids' book of kaleidoscopes / by Carolyn Bennett with Jack Romig.
p.   cm.
ISBN 1-56305-638-0
1. Kaleidoscope—Juvenile literature. 2. Kaleidoscope—Equipment and supplies—Juvenile literature. 3. Toy and movable books—Specimens. [1. Kaleidoscope. 2.Handicraft. 3. Toy and movable books.] I. Romig, Jack. II. Title.
QC373.K3B46 1994
535'.078—dc20
94–27253 CIP AC

Design by Lisa Hollander
Photo Credits: Pages 3 & 45, courtesy of Cozy Baker; pages 1, 5, 23, 24, 58, 61, 75, & 78 courtesy of Carolyn Bennett; pages 11 & 12 by Walt Chrynwski; page 40, honeycomb © Treat Davidson/Photo Researchers, Inc., snowflake © Nuridsany et Perennou/Science Source/Photo Researchers, Inc., diatoms © M.I. Walker/Science Source/Photo Researchers, Inc.; page 41, Sheilah Scully; page 43, quilt by Afton Germany courtesy of Robert Cargo Folk Art Gallery, Tuscaloosa, Alabama. All other photography by John Bean (photo stylist Lori S. Malkin).

Workman books are available at special discounts when purchased in bulk for premiums and sales promotions as well as for fund-raising or educational use. Special editions or book excerpts can also be created to specification. For details, contact the Special Sales Director at the address below.

Workman Publishing Company, Inc.
708 Broadway
New York, NY 10003

Manufactured in the United States of America

First Printing October 1994
10 9 8 7 6 5 4 3 2

DEDICATION

This book is dedicated to my parents: my mother, Bertha, who has always been a loving and artistic inspiration and who has unconditionally supported my every effort; and my late father, Arnold, who taught me that tools can be fun and that making things with my hands is extremely rewarding.

ACKNOWLEDGMENTS

SPECIAL THANKS:

To Cozy Baker for her friendship and her endless enthusiasm for kaleidoscopes.

To my sister, Beverly, and her family, with my appreciation and love.

To the staff of C. Bennett Scopes for their loyalty and help.

To Jack Romig for his excellent writing and research.

To Anne Kostick for her great assistance and exciting ideas.

To Lisa Hollander and Lori S. Malkin, the design team at Workman Publishing.

To my fellow scopemakers for the inventiveness and creativity that makes the kaleidoscope community such a delight.

And last but not least, to my husband Barry Kramer for the love and joy he has brought to my life.

Contents

INTRODUCTION

DISCOVERING SCOPES..1
SCOPE HISTORY 3
SCOPE ASSEMBLY 6

SCOPE SCIENCE

Light.................................10

REFLECTING ON THE NATURE OF LIGHT • THE LAKE IN THE SKY • *A New Angle on Seeing* • **FOCUSING ON LENSES** • *Glassy Gazes* • **WHY PEOPLE WEAR GLASSES • THE SMOOTHEST BOUNCE** • *Through the Looking Glass* • *Multiply Your Money With Mirrors* • **MAKING MIRRORS** • *Hall of mirrors* • **KALEIDOSCOPE REFLECTIONS • THE WORLD IS YOUR OBJECT CHAMBER**

Color 25

A RAINBOW UNDER WRAPS • *Breaking Out the Colors* • **WHAT'S REALLY IN YOUR PAINTBOX?** • **CREATING FILTERED LIGHT** • **FANCY SUNGLASSES** • *Polarvision*

Symmetry................34

PLANE AND SIMPLE • *Your Two-faced Family* •
OTHER KINDS OF SYMMETRY • *Paper-folded Symmetry*
• **SYMMETRY IN NATURE** • **ARTS AND CRAFTS** •
Kaleido-drawings

SCOPE ART

A Kaleido-Comeback.....44

Becoming a Scopemaster.46

A SCOPEMASTER'S KIT • A SCOPEMASTER'S MATERIALS

PROJECT: A COLOR-WHEEL SCOPE......................52

PROJECT: MORE WHEELS.....................................54

PROJECT: SCRIBBLE SCOPE................................58

PROJECT: HOLY TELEIDO.....................................60

PROJECT: CHIP SCOPE...62

PROJECT: SQUISHY SCOPES................................65

PROJECT: FLASHLIGHT SCOPE............................68

PROJECT: OTHER MIRRORS.................................70

PROJECT: FURTHER REFLECTION........................72

PROJECT: SHADOW SCOPES...............................76

PROJECT: A MIRRORED TUNNEL.........................77

PROJECT: POLARIZING SCOPES..........................78

PROJECT: ROCKET SCOPE..................................80

PROJECT: TELEIDOSNAP!....................................82

**DECORATION IDEAS • HOLDERS AND STANDS •
SOURCES • SHAPES TO TRACE**

Discovering
Scopes

The kaleidoscope can be a simple device—as simple as a cardboard tube, two or three mirrors and some pieces of plastic. But when you put the pieces together just right, the kaleidoscope becomes a peephole into a magic world. All at once it reveals a blizzard of

Here are a few of the many kaleidoscopes I've designed.

colored snowflakes, a tube full of fireworks, a handful of stars.

I let my first kaleidoscope get away. When I was a child, I visited the Corning Glass Works in upstate New York with my family. The factory there was full of amazing objects made of glass. When the tour was over, my parents let me pick out a souvenir at the gift shop. I handled a pretty kaleidoscope, then chose something else. But I never forgot the scope at Corning.

Back home, I found instructions in an old encyclopedia for building one of my own. The language was old-fashioned—"A Kaleidoscope a Boy Can Make," it said. (Of course, a girl could make one too.) The scope worked surprisingly well.

After that I was hooked. I collected scopes and learned about their history and the science behind them. I invented more scopes of my own, learning how to make the picture in the tube brighter and livelier. Eventually I started my own business, creating and selling scopes. That was 20 years ago, and I'm still excited about kaleidoscopes.

This book is my chance to share my excitement, to show you what kaleidoscopes can do, and what you can do with kaleidoscopes.

Scope History

The kaleidoscope sparkled first in the imagination of Sir David Brewster, a scientist born in Edinburgh, Scotland, in 1781. Brewster spent his life studying the principles of light, and his hard work was rewarded by many discoveries. (His designs for lighthouses, for instance, saved the lives of thousands of sailors.)

Brewster was most interested in what happened when light was reflected, or bounced off, an object. Nothing he did brought so much fame to himself or so much pleasure to others as his invention of the kaleidoscope, which works because of light reflection.

The idea behind the kaleidoscope wasn't new, even in Brewster's day. Ptolemy, a Greek mathematician who lived almost 2,000 years ago, had written about a surprising thing that happened when two or more reflecting

An antique kaleidoscope on a stand, designed by Brewster.

WHAT'S IN A NAME?

When Brewster developed the kaleidoscope, he followed the fashion of his time in choosing a name. Educated people of a century or two ago were expected to know Latin, the language of ancient Rome, as well as Greek.

To name his toy, Brewster put together three Greek words: *kalos*, beautiful; *eidos*, form; and *skopeo*, I see. So kaleidoscope really means "I see a beautiful form."

surfaces (such as mirrors) came together.

What caught Ptolemy's eye was the multiplication of images. A single mirror reflects one image—one "picture" of an object in front of it. You might think that two mirrors would reflect just two images, but in this case one plus one equals something unexpected.

Depending on the angle between two mirrors, a viewer might see three reflections of an object in front of them. Or five. Or seven. Or, if the mirrors are directly facing each other, an endless parade of reflections. The repeated reflections are arranged in a pattern we call symmetrical. That means one side of the view perfectly balances the other.

Brewster saw that the patterns made by bouncing light could be impressive—even beautiful. His next inspiration was to add color and movement to the reflections revealed by his two mirrors.

He put the mirrors in a tube, added a clear box called an object chamber to one end of the tube, trapped bits of colored, broken glass in the chamber, and worked out a way to make the chamber turn. When he looked through the tube, he said that "the succession of splendid colors formed a phenomenon which could be considered as one of the most beautiful in optics."

He described it thoroughly in his 174-page *Treatise on the Kaleidoscope.* In his book he calculated that 24 pieces of glass in a kaleidoscope could be combined in 1,391,724,288,887, 252,999,425,128,493,402,200 ways. He also explained how to build a scope, where to put the eyepiece, even how to choose the best color combinations. Compared to writing his book, building a model of the invention was easy—maybe it was too easy. The kaleidoscope was a roaring success, and more than 200,000 were sold within a few months after Brewster filed his patent. Unfortunately for him, many were sold by companies that paid nothing for the use of his invention. Popular as it was, it earned him little money, and he wasted years defending his rights as its inventor.

Brewster, a practical man, thought of the kaleidoscope mainly as a tool to help designers. True, kaleidoscopes have given us a new way of seeing, and from them have come new and beautiful designs for buildings, books, rugs, jewelry and much more. But the world loved his invention mostly as a toy, an amusement for children and adults.

To really understand what Brewster (and millions of people since) found so pleasing, you need a working kaleidoscope of your own.

Scope Assembly

Start by clearing a work space on a counter or table. Spread the parts of your scope out in front of you. Check each part against the pictures on these pages to make sure you have everything you'll need. Three squares of cellophane are also included, but you won't need them right away. Just set them to one side for now.

▲ A short tube that will form the turning end, or object chamber, of your scope.

▲ An end cap of frosted, flexible plastic.

▲ A long tube, which is the body of the scope. A disk with a hole in the center is fitted into one end. This is your eyepiece. (If your scope's disk is loose in the tube or package, insert it before step 1.)

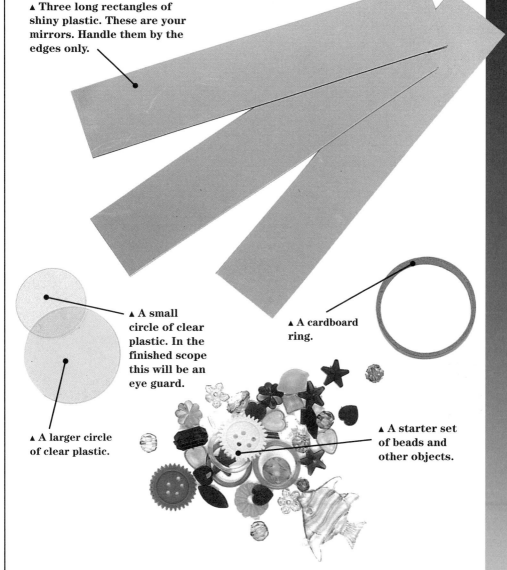

▲ Three long rectangles of shiny plastic. These are your mirrors. Handle them by the edges only.

▲ A small circle of clear plastic. In the finished scope this will be an eye guard.

▲ A cardboard ring.

▲ A larger circle of clear plastic.

▲ A starter set of beads and other objects.

As you follow the assembly steps on the next pages, the mirrors, tubes and rings may seem to be a tight fit. This is intentional, and will give you a better image in the finished scope.

1. Drop the eye guard (the smaller circle) into the long tube. The eye guard must lie flat against the inside of the eyepiece; you may have to shake the tube a bit to get it flat. It should cover the hole in the eyepiece so nothing can fall into your eye. No matter what kind of scope you're making, always be sure this piece is in place.

2. Now slide the mirrors into the tube. HANDLE THE MIRRORS BY THE EDGES ONLY; try to avoid any scratches or fingerprints. Slide one mirror into the tube. Slide in the second mirror, making a "V" of the two mirrors as you look at them from one end. Add the third mirror; it should cross the top of the "V" to form a triangle, with the mirrors facing *in*.

Stop for a minute to look through the eyepiece. Wiggle your fingers at the other end. How many fingers do you see? Now turn the tube around and look through the open end. You should see a cluster of holes—multiplied reflections of the eyepiece.

3. Next, find the shorter tube. This is the scope's object chamber. Slip it onto the scope from the eyepiece end. The end of the chamber that has an *un*rolled edge goes on first. Slide the chamber all the way up the tube until it is stopped by the tube's outer ring.

4. Peel off the protective film from both sides of the large clear plastic circle, drop it into the open end of the chamber, and gently press it down against the end of the tube. Try not to leave any fingerprints on the disk.

5. Now fit the cardboard ring into the open end of the object chamber.

6. Put some or all of the colored beads and objects from your kit into the object chamber, then fit the end cap tightly into the chamber.

Now, look! Your kaleidoscope shows a unique picture that changes each time you turn the chamber. Already you can start thinking in new ways about the art and science of light.

Light

When you look into your kaleidoscope, you're not really seeing beads or marbles or other shapes. What you're seeing is light.

Light is so much a part of our world that we usually take it for granted. That doesn't make it any less important—or any less mysterious. All vision depends on it. It acts in ways we might never imagine, even though it surrounds us all our lives, and we see it every day.

The way light behaves is crucial to the working of kaleidoscopes. In fact, it's crucial to the way everything in the world looks to us.

REFLECTING ON THE NATURE OF LIGHT

For as long as people have been thinking scientifically about light, they've been wondering what it's really like. Does it move in a flow like the ripples of water in a pond? Or is it like a bunch of little balls tossed off in all directions from its source? To ask the question as scientists do: Is light made up of waves or particles?

The answer is yes! Depending on what experiments we try, light can behave like the waves in water or like zillions of little packets of energy, or like both at the same time.

But when we think about how kaleidoscopes work, what's really important is that light bounces. We call this bouncing effect reflection. It happens with both particles and waves.

Without reflection, there would be no kaleidoscopes. In fact, without reflection, we couldn't see anything unless it was luminous—gave off light of its own, like the sun or a light bulb.

Here's how reflection works. Whenever light hits a surface, some of it gets soaked up, or absorbed, and its energy makes the surface warmer. (You've felt this when you've touched a dark-colored object that's been left in the sun on a hot summer day.)

*L*ight waves coming from the light bulb bounce, or reflect, off the angled white card into the girl's face. Holding the card at a different angle would aim the reflected light somewhere else.

Many of the light waves bounce back off again. When the light hits straight on, it bounces straight off (if the surface is perfectly flat and smooth). If the light hits at an angle, it elbows off at the same angle from the surface.

That reflected light is what we see when we look at any object that doesn't shine with its own light. Sunshine or lamplight bounces off a tree, a car, your dog or this page, and some of that light reaches your eye. The sensors inside the eye send a message to your brain, which puts together a picture based on the message.

THE LAKE IN THE SKY

Everybody has seen mirages in cartoons: After days in the desert, the flannel-tongued traveler sees a beautiful oasis. But as soon as he reaches it, it disappears.

Sometimes people really are fooled by mirages. It's a simple matter of refraction. Light bouncing from visible objects high above the ground—such as treetops, clouds and other parts of the sky—is bent when it passes from a layer of cool air high in the atmosphere to a hotter layer at ground level.

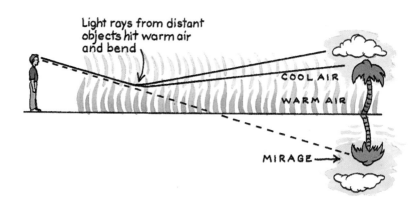

Light rays from distant objects hit warm air and bend

COOL AIR

WARM AIR

MIRAGE

A NEW ANGLE ON SEEING

— — —

Reflection is just one of the surprising ways light moves through our world. A simple experiment that you can try in your kitchen will show you another way that light behaves. You'll need an assistant and three props: a teacup, a quarter and a pitcher of water.

Put the quarter in the cup. Station yourself near the rim, with your eyes at a level where you can see inside the cup, but the coin is just out of sight. Have your helper fill the cup with water—slowly, so that the quarter isn't disturbed.

Don't move your head as the water pours in. You won't need to: As the cup fills, the quarter will come into view.

Did it float to the top? Of course not—it's too heavy! If your assistant did the job right it hasn't even moved. Why can you see it now?

Sometimes the light that reaches your eye hasn't traveled along a straight path. Light can be bent when it passes from one substance to another—in your experiment, from the air to the water and back again. This bending is called refraction.

When you looked into the empty cup you were seeing only the light from its inside wall. But the addition of water bent the light bouncing off the bottom of the cup (where the quarter was) until it bounced into your eye.

1. Put the quarter in the cup and station yourself near the rim.

2. Don't move your head as the water pours in.

3. As the cup fills, the quarter will come into view.

It looks to us as if we're seeing an upside-down tree, a cloud and a patch of sky on the desert floor—because we believe we're seeing light coming into our eyes in a straight line. The real blue of the refracted sky looks like a lake. The tree and cloud look as if they're reflected in the lake.

FOCUSING ON LENSES

Light can be bent by anything it passes through—a bottle of apple juice, a glass of water, hot air rising from a road in summer, a marble. Maybe the best tool for bending light is a lens, which is made just for the job.

The word "lens" comes from another Latin root; originally it meant "lentil." Some lenses are the same shape as a lentil: round, thin around the edge and thick in the center.

This outward-bulging lens is called a convex lens. Convex lenses bend light in toward the center of the lens. Somewhere behind every convex lens is a place where those rays of light come together. That's called the focal point. The distance from the lens to the focal point is the focal length.

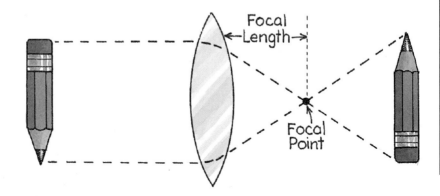

Focal
←Length→

Focal
Point

GLASSY GAZES

— — —

Curved glass, like water, changes the direction of light, sometimes with surprising results.

As an example, look at a friend through a large, clear glass of water. Your friend's face will appear enlarged, reversed, or misshapen. It might even disappear, depending on the way the light is bent.

With two magnifying lenses you can flip a magnified image upside down. First, look at a picture through one lens, moving the lens until the magnified image appears in focus. Then add the second lens in between the first one and your eye. Slowly moving one or both lenses, you'll find a spot where the magnified image you see through both lenses appears upside down. And because of the extra curving of two lenses, the image you see will also appear more "curved" than through only one lens.

WHY PEOPLE WEAR GLASSES

You carry a pair of convex lenses around with you all the time—the lenses of your eyes.

These lenses, called corneas, make it possible for you to see clearly. At the back of your eye is the retina, a sensitive membrane covered with special cells that receive light and convert it into messages your brain can understand. Without lenses, the world would be a blur.

If the focus falls short of the back of the eye, a person is nearsighted, and can't see far-away things well. If the focus is behind the eye, as in this picture, the person is farsighted, and has trouble focusing on things close up.

The cornea works the same way as other lenses. When light passes through it, it's bent. If you have perfect vision, your cornea aims the images to fall right on your retina. If you wear eyeglasses, you are putting another lens between your corneas and the things you see. The new lens bends the light before it gets to your cornea. When it reaches your eye, the second bending from your cornea puts the image where it belongs—on your retina.

With or without glasses, the image formed on your retina is always upside down. So why doesn't everything look like you're standing on your head?

The answer is that your brain is so accustomed to upside-down images that it interprets them as right side up. The world looks right to you because your brain is so good at understanding it.

THE SMOOTHEST BOUNCE

Take a minute to examine your mirrors. You'll see that the surfaces are *very* smooth. That smoothness is what makes them good mirrors.

The more uneven a surface is, the more it scatters reflected light. Most objects have fairly rough surfaces—even a page in this book is rough—so that light hops off in lots of directions. However, we still get enough reflected light from the objects to be able to see them.

But a mirror is different. Because it's extremely smooth, it reflects almost all the light that touches it without much scattering. (Other smooth surfaces, such as a shiny button or the chrome detail on a car, work the same way.) The light bounces off the mirror in the same pattern as it arrived from the object. As a result, you don't see the surface of the mirror so much as you see the reflection in the mirror.

▲ **The bagel is opaque. Light waves coming from the far side of the toaster cannot pass through.**

▲ **The glass is translucent. Some light can pass through, so we can see the orange juice. But some light is blocked, so we also see the surface of the glass.**

▲ **The bowl is transparent. Almost all the light from the berries passes through and reaches our eyes.**

▲ **The toaster is reflective. Light from the juice glass and the berry bowl bounces straight back, giving us a clear virtual image of breakfast.**

The picture in the mirror is called a virtual image. When you look into a mirror, everything inside it looks just as "deep" as the real world on your side of the glass. If you stand five feet from the mirror, your reflection appears to be ten feet away from you—that is, five feet *into* the mirror.

THROUGH THE LOOKING GLASS

— — —

That reflection you smirk at in the mirror—it looks just like you, doesn't it?

Well, not quite. Wink at it. If you shut your left eye, the reflection stubbornly closes its right. Hold up your watch—the second hand on the reflection's watch goes backward!

Put on your favorite T-shirt, and the lettering on the reflection's shirt is reversed, almost unreadable. But you can have the last laugh.

Write your laugh—"OHO"—on a piece of paper. Now hold it up for the reflection to see. The paper in the reflection's hand still says "OHO"! That's because the word is symmetrical—the same on the left of the center as on the right.

But for mirror writing to work, all the letters have to be symmetrical from left to right. (You can use A, H, I, M, O, T, U, V, W, X and Y.) And that's not all. The words and sentences also have to be symmetrical; that means they must be spelled the same way forward and backward. TOT, TOOT, HAH and YAY will work.

Or, think of words spelled only with letters that are symmetrical from top to bottom—B, C, D, E, H, I, K, O and X. (The numbers 0, 1, 3 and 8 work, too.) Write a sentence using only these words. If you hold the page upside down when you look in the mirror you'll still be able to read it as if it were right side up.

If you put a small, unframed mirror on "OHO" so that it divides the H down the middle, you'll still be able to read it.

Send a message to your mother with "WOW MOM WOW."

MULTIPLY YOUR MONEY WITH MIRRORS

■ ■ ■

Place two of your kit mirrors at a 90-degree angle (see angle guide on page 75). Put a dime in the corner, head side up. Now you should see four dimes. Look at the dime in each mirror. The inscription reads "YTЯƎᗺI⅃." Now look at the dime that's formed across the corner between the two mirrors. Although it's upside down compared to the original dime, the lettering on the coin's image reads just like the original—"LIBERTY."

Why? Because the dime in the corner is not a direct reflection of the original coin, but a reflection of a reflection. The image you see is the reverse of the first reversed reflection, so it looks as if it's back to normal.

Now change the angle of the mirrors so that you see six complete dimes. You'll see them arranged in a circle. In fact, twin mirrors give us a good way to divide circles into equal parts—in this case, six.

Continue changing the angle between the mirrors to make more or fewer dimes. Easy come, easy go.

1. When the two mirrors are angled just right, you'll see four dimes.

2. Look closely to see the lettering on the three reflected dimes.

3. By moving the mirrors closer together you can increase the number of dimes.

MAKING MIRRORS

The secret of mirror-making is thousands of years old. The first mirrors were plates of polished metal. Even when glassmakers learned how to create a fairly clear glass mirror with a back covering of tin or lead, bubbles and waves in the glass distorted the reflected image.

Better mirrors came along with the development of plate glass—large, flat sheets—with good reflective backing called silvering or foiling.

With plate glass mirrors the light must first pass *through* the glass before it's reflected. Remember, the reflective surface is on the back side of the glass. Light is bent, or refracted, by the glass, and the viewer doesn't get a completely true image.

Although the plain glass reflects some light, the addition of shiny foil makes it far more reflective.

Polished metal mirrors like those of ancient times would be better for a kaleidoscope because the light reflects off the top surface without passing through glass. Your scope includes just this kind of "first-surface" mirror, with reflections coming off the top.

THE HALL OF MIRRORS

— — —

For this experiment you will need two large mirrors and an adult to help you hold them. One way to do this is to take a framed mirror into the bathroom so that you can also use the mirror attached to the medicine cabinet.

Set the mirrors up facing each other. You'll find that you've created a long tunnel of reflections. As the light bounces back and forth between mirrors, the images shrink down almost to nothing and become more faint with every bounce.

These are called converging reflections, and they come with some surprising math built in. Every one of the reflections is twice the size of the next one farther in. And if you could stack them all up, they would be just about twice as high as the tallest reflection.

KALEIDOSCOPE REFLECTIONS

It is the arrangement of mirrors inside a kaleidoscope that determines what the view will be like. Since your kit scope uses three mirrors, you're staring down a little triangular tunnel at the object chamber when you look through the eyepiece.

It doesn't look like just one triangle, though, does it? Instead, you see a repeated pattern of triangles covering the whole viewing area.

What accounts for this picture? Light entering the scope from outside passes through the object chamber. The light bounces off some things in the chamber and passes through others. Some of the light goes straight to your eye—and that's the first of the triangular areas you see.

Remember our experiment with the mirrors and the dime? The triangle we're talking about now corresponds to the real dime. You may be able to spot this first wedge. If you hold the object chamber still and turn the barrel of the scope, it will be the one that seems to move the least—all the other sections seem to move around it. In some scopes, it will also be the brightest one.

Not all of the light entering the scope made it straight to your eye. Some of it bounced off the things in the object chamber, hit the three mirrors inside the scope and was reflected directly from them to your eye. That makes three more wedges in the pattern—one for each mirror.

This is the first wedge.

Some light, instead of bouncing from the mirror to your eye, was reflected instead from mirror to mirror before it got to your eye—and those triangular images are the ones that fill in the rest of the scope picture.

THE WORLD IS YOUR OBJECT CHAMBER

The number of things you can put into your object chamber is limited only by size. But you don't have to look only at objects that fit inside. If you take the cap off your scope, you have an entirely new instrument called a teleidoscope.

The teleidoscope is another invention of Sir David Brewster. He called it teleidoscope because the idea was to look far away— and "tele" means "far" in Greek.

With your scope rigged this way, you can point it at anything— and whatever object you choose will be broken into a series of reflections.

With a teleidoscope it's especially easy to spot the "first triangle" we discussed in the previous section. But in this special scope, the other triangles are likely to look very different than that patch of direct light— especially if the objects you view are far away. If you look at objects close up, the teleidoscope view will be more like what you see through a kaleidoscope, with each of the triangles very similar to one another. See page 60 for more ideas about this special scope.

Color

Just like light itself, the familiar color of our world is more complicated than it seems.

Wherever we look, the things we see are full of color. Or are they? Actually, most of the color we see is really another trick of light.

Think about some of the most colorful things you know, such as paint, crayons and jelly beans. The big surprise is that color doesn't exist in any of them.

Now think about a beam of light. That white light is made up of every color we see in the rainbow.

A RAINBOW UNDER WRAPS

The colors of the rainbow hide in plain sight all the time. The first scientist to realize this was Sir Isaac Newton, an Englishman who lived during the 1600s.

In his experiment, Newton passed white sunlight through a triangular glass shape called a prism. The light splintered into a pattern of pure colors—red, orange, yellow, green, blue, indigo and violet, in that order. When people looked at the array of colors—called a spectrum—most assumed that something in the glass had changed the light to give it color. But Newton understood that the prism had only separated the white light into colors that were there all along.

To understand this, think of light as a wave. Different colors of light "wave" more or less often as they cover the same distance. Another way of saying this is that the colors have different wavelengths.

Red light has longer wavelengths, violet light has shorter ones. The wavelengths of the other colors fall between these two.

When these mixed wavelengths pass through a prism, the long waves of red light are bent the least. The shorter waves of violet light bend the most. All the colors bend differently, and as they do, they separate. A spectrum is created.

LIGHT

White light from the left side of this crystal is bent as it travels through the glass, creating spectrum color surrounded by a shadow. Light coming from other directions may create flashes of color against the sides of the crystal.

BREAKING OUT THE COLORS

— — —

You can create a spectrum if you have a plastic tray or tub and a glass mirror. Don't use your kit mirrors. Try this experiment in a room where lots of sunlight comes through a window, or use a flashlight.

Fill the tray with water. Set your mirror in the water at about the angle shown in the photograph. Move the tray in the sunlight, or move the flashlight beam around, aiming the flash of reflected light at a white wall, card or piece of paper. The spectrum should appear on the white surface.

The water works just like a prism, breaking up white light. The colors in the light are separated so that you can see them.

You'll find that flash of spectrum colors in lots of places—in a patch of oil floating on a wet driveway, on the surface of compact disks, in soap bubbles. Whenever you see it, remember that the colors are really in the light.

WHAT'S REALLY IN YOUR PAINT BOX?

Now that we've seen where color is, let's think about where it isn't. It *isn't* in a box of watercolor paints.

What's really in there is a selection of light-absorbing materials called pigments, mixed with some other material that helps you apply the paint. When you use the paint, it seems as if you're just covering a surface with the color you've chosen. What looks like color in your paint box is just another example of light reflection.

Let's say you're painting a picture of the American flag on a piece of white paper. You start with the red stripes. You've put down pigment that soaks up every color in white light except red. The red light bounces off, and that's the color the stripes appear to be.

When you paint the blue part of the flag, the paint we call blue reflects blue light and absorbs the other colors, so it appears blue.

The stars and the rest of the stripes are unpainted. Because they absorb *none* of the spectrum colors and reflect *all* the colors, they appear to be white.

If you try mixing paints, you'll get combinations of pigments that absorb and reflect different colors. For instance, put yellow and blue pigments together and you'll get green. That's because the mixed pigments for those colors absorb all the wavelengths in white light *except* for those in the green range.

▲ **Mixing cyan and yellow absorbs everything but green.**

▲ **Yellow pigment absorbs blue light and reflects red and green light.**

▲ **Cyan pigment absorbs red light and reflects green and blue light.**

▲ **Mixing yellow and magenta absorbs everything but red.**

▲ **Mixing magenta and cyan absorbs everything but blue.**

▲ **Magenta pigment absorbs green light and reflects red and blue light.**

▲ **A perfect mix of colors would absorb all light and appear black.**

The color wheel shows how mixing pigments can make most of the colors in nature. Yellow, magenta and cyan are basic for this kind of color creation, so we call them the primary colors, even though it all works by *adding* pigments—not colors—to *subtract* light.

Suppose you mixed all your pigments together. You'd get something that looks like dark mud. That mixture has so many pigments that it subtracts almost all the visible wavelengths. If the absorption was perfect, your everything-but-the-kitchen-sink mixture would be black, reflecting no light at all.

CREATING
FILTERED LIGHT

Inside your kaleidoscope's object chamber, any object that doesn't transmit or absorb light reflects it. In this kind of scope, objects that don't transmit light reveal mostly shape to your eye, showing up as silhouettes, or dark outlines.

The kaleidoscope doesn't mix pigments, but it does give you a chance to look at another way color becomes visible.

When white light passes through a piece of colored cellophane like the ones in the kit, the cellophane knocks out some of the colors. If you hold your red cellophane between a source of white light and a white piece of paper, you'll see a red "shadow" on the paper. The cellophane has blocked the other colors in white light, and red is all that's left to pass through and bounce off the paper to your eye.

When you put cellophane over the end of the object chamber, you subtract all the colors in white light except the color of the cellophane. Objects in the chamber will look like the color of the cellophane if they reflect or transmit light in those wavelengths, or will look dark if they don't.

FANCY SUNGLASSES

Polarized light can create unusual effects in your kaleidoscope. To understand it, think again about the wave theory of light.

The squiggle on this page isn't a very good picture of a light wave. The vibrating particle that creates the wave isn't moving just up and down, as the squiggle would suggest. It moves in all directions.

This squiggle shows how light waves may travel in one direction. The girl shaking the rope can make the wave travel from her to the boy— as long as the wave can pass through the slots in the chair back.

POLARVISION

— — —

If you or your parents have an old, discarded pair of plastic polarizing sunglasses, you can use them to see how effective they are at blocking light.

Take the lenses out of the sunglass frames. (You may need an adult's help for this.) Hold one lens, by its edge, in each hand. Line them up in front of your eye. Twist one hand so that one lens rotates while the other lens remains still. Twist slowly, looking through both lenses.

You'll see the brightness change drastically. In one position, there should be plenty of light coming through; in another, almost none.

When you see light through the lenses, the polarizing filters are lined up in the same direction—the "slots" in both filters run the same way, so they'll allow light through. But when you turn the first filter 90 degrees (a quarter of the way around), the second filter stops all the light that came through the first one. Then you can't see anything.

A simple experiment makes this easier to imagine. Have a friend hold one end of a jump rope or a long piece of string. Gently shake your end of the rope while your friend holds the other end still. You can make a kind of wave pass from you to your friend. If you move the rope up and down, you get a wave that looks like the squiggle on the page. But you can make waves to the left and right, and at any other angle, depending on which way you move the rope. Like your rope, light can move in any direction along the path it travels.

Now suppose you pass the rope through something that stops it from moving in all directions, such as a slatted chair back. If you move the rope up and down, the waves still reach your friend. If you move the rope from side to side, they don't.

A polarizing filter does the same thing. At the beach, where light reflects off the sand and water, our eyes may get ten times as much light as we need. This is called glare, and a lot of it is light that vibrates in horizontal directions. By wearing sunglasses made with polarizing lenses set to allow only vertical vibrations to pass through, we shut out most of that painful glare, making it easier to see.

BREWSTER'S 3-D SCOPE

David Brewster's stereoscope was another popular toy in Victorian homes.

It used a viewer and a pair of nearly identical photos on a card.

The two slightly different photos imitated the different viewing positions of our two eyes. The stereoscope used special lenses which bent the light coming from the two photos; to the eyes, the light seemed to come from only one place. The brain combined the separate photos into one image, giving the illusion of depth.

Symmetry

Remember when you tried mirror writing? It worked because of symmetry, which is a kind of balance we see in the construction or arrangement of things.

An amazing number of objects in nature, science and art are symmetrical. Whenever you look into your kaleidoscope you see symmetry, because opposite parts of the view balance one another. A kaleidoscope creates many kinds of symmetry from reflected images.

PLANE AND SIMPLE

One object that shows natural symmetry is the human body. Think about it while you look at yourself in a mirror. You'll see pairs of eyes, ears, nostrils, arms, hands, legs and feet. If you could look inside, you'd see the same pattern repeated in many of your inner parts. Your brain is divided into two halves called hemispheres. You have two lungs and two kidneys.

Lay your hands, palms down, on a table. They're *not* exactly alike, are they? Your left hand has the thumb to the right, pinkie on the left. Your right hand? Just the reverse.

This is a special symmetry that's part of your body. It's like the symmetry between a real object and its mirror image. To prove this to yourself, try placing just your left hand on the table. Set up a mirror next to it. You'll see that the reflected hand looks very much like your right hand.

The surface of the mirror is like a wall between your hand and its reflection. The symmetry between the hand and the image balances along that make-believe wall. And because we call a flat surface a plane, this kind of symmetry is called plane symmetry. It's exactly the same kind of symmetry that exists between the paired parts of your body.

The reflection of your left hand looks just like your right hand, and vice versa.

YOUR TWO-FACED FAMILY

Check out your face in the mirror. Draw an imaginary vertical line down the middle. It probably will look about the same on both sides, but chances are the left and right sides are a little different.

Want to prove it? You'll need one of your kit mirrors and any picture of a person's face—photos of friends or relatives or pictures from newspapers and magazines. Try to find pictures in which the person is looking straight at the camera.

Put the edge of your mirror on the picture so that it divides the face in half from the top of the head to the chin. Look first at one side of the face with that side reflected in the mirror. Now turn the mirror around and look at the other side of the face in the same way.

The faces may look like they belong to two different people. That's because the symmetry between the two halves of real faces is close, but not exact. When you use the mirror in this way, the reflection makes each side of the face exactly like the other—so what you see for either half of the face may be very different from the original picture.

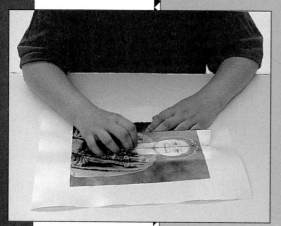

OTHER KINDS OF SYMMETRY

Flat images often show a balance called line symmetry. Familiar shapes including circles, squares and triangles display this kind of symmetry. There's a simple test for line symmetry. If you can fold a picture along a line so that the resulting halves match up exactly, then line symmetry is present.

Still another kind of symmetry can exist without a simple dividing line. Think of looking down on a table set for four, as in the photograph below.

There's no way to draw a line that splits the tabletop into halves that are alike. But the picture you see still has symmetry.

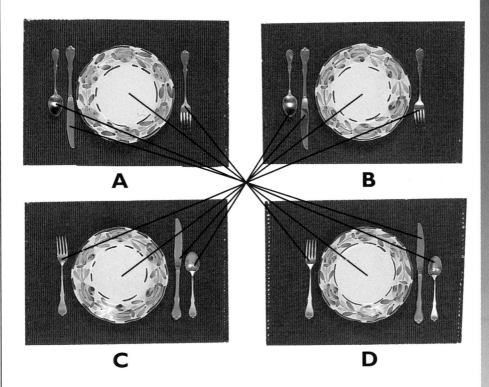

The lines on the picture show how the fork at plate C balances the fork at plate B. In fact, everything at plate C matches up with something like it at plate B. The same thing is true if you compare plates A and D.

Notice that the lines that connect the matching parts all cross at one point. That's why we say the tabletop has point symmetry.

To see if a small object or picture has point symmetry, just turn it halfway around. If it looks exactly the same, it has point symmetry.

PAPER-FOLDED SYMMETRY

— — —

Fold a square piece of paper from corner to corner, making a triangle. Cut interesting shapes out of the folded edge, leaving some of the fold uncut. When you unfold it you'll have a pattern with line symmetry. Now fold a new square the same way, and then fold it in half again. Cut a pattern along the two folded sides of the triangle, again leaving parts of the fold. Now your square has four-part symmetry.

If you fold the triangle a third time before cutting, you'll get symmetry that divides the square into eight parts. It has line symmetry along the first fold you made and in other directions as well. If you are still able to cut the paper after you fold it four times, your pattern will appear in 16 parts.

One fold, top left; two folds, top right; three folds, bottom left; four folds, bottom right. The more folds in the paper, the more ways in which the design is symmetrical.

SYMMETRY IN NATURE

Humans aren't alone in being constructed along symmetrical lines. If you have a cat, hamster, parakeet, turtle, goldfish or almost any other animal as a pet, you should be able to imagine a plane that would divide it into nearly identical halves.

In simpler animals and plants, the symmetry can be even easier to spot. Many sea creatures have twin shells that open and shut—shells that can be as alike as the two covers of a book. The arms of a sea star often give a clear display of symmetry.

When bees build their honeycombs, they use for the

cells a six-sided symmetrical form called a hexagon. Not only is this a very strong shape, it also allows for the most storage room within the available space. Among plants, symmetry can be seen in countless places. Many leaves have mirror-image symmetry.

Microscopic sea plants called diatoms have radial symmetry—like the spokes of a wheel—which looks delicate, but is really very strong. The most beautiful diatoms look like the stained-glass "rose" windows in great churches.

A honeycomb.

An arrangement of diatoms.

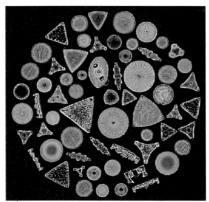

Crystals are still another part of the natural world rich in symmetry. A snowflake, for instance, is really an ice crystal with a complicated structure so tiny that you may not be able to see it at all.

A snowflake.

Each snowflake begins with molecules of water high in the atmosphere. Because each water molecule has three atoms—two of hydrogen and one of oxygen—it forms a triangle with three equal sides.

New crystals grow from the point of the triangle as the water turns to ice. When six of the triangles have formed together, they make up a hexagon. Then, as the six-sided ice crystal falls through the air, its sides become the framework for more growth.

By the time it reaches the ground any number of elaborate forms may have taken shape. Snowflakes can be shaped like plain columns, columns with caps on either end, needles, flat plates, stars or like the familiar lacy designs we call snowflake patterns.

Animal, vegetable or mineral, the list of objects and living things with some sort of symmetrical structure is almost endless. Prove this to yourself by taking a nature walk. See how many examples of symmetry you can find in the park or the backyard.

ARTS AND CRAFTS

A stained-glass rose window.

When people began to make things with their hands, whether useful objects for everyday living or works of art, they often made symmetry a part of what they did.

Sometimes sym-metry has been cho-sen just because it works so well. A skilled woodworker of long ago might have built a four-legged table—which could show plane symme-

KALEIDO-DRAWINGS

To draw a kaleidoscopic design, trace a large circle onto a piece of tracing paper and cut it out. Fold the circle in half once, then twice more, and draw your picture on the top wedge of the folded circle.

Open up the circle so that it's folded just once, then flip it over and retrace your original design onto the opposite wedge of the paper. Now fold the paper one time, flip it over, and trace onto the blank wedge. Keep refolding and flipping the paper disk until you've traced the pattern on each of the eight wedges.

Now color in the design. To keep it really kaleidoscopic, repeat the same color for the same parts of the design in each of the eight sections.

try, depending on its shape—mostly because a table made that way is extremely sturdy.

Some people think one of the reasons that symmetry in the arts is so powerful is that it *isn't* always just like something in nature. Because these patterns are new, they can have a powerful effect on our imaginations and emotions.

Religious art has used symmetrical forms for thousands of years. Never mind that a cathedral's rose window looks like an ocean plant—the people who made the window had never seen a diatom. What they did with color and balance was not so much to mirror the world as to help people look far beyond it.

The skilled use of symmetry

This beautiful pieced quilt shows several kinds of human-designed symmetry.

in the arts can be dazzling, whether it's part of a Star of Bethlehem quilt or a modern painting. When you make a kaleidoscope, you open a window into that same special way of seeing.

SCOPE ART

A Kaleido-Comeback

The idea that the kaleidoscope itself is a work of art isn't new. In the Victorian era (named for Queen Victoria, who ruled England during much of the 1800s), a kaleidoscope might have been displayed on a stand like a small telescope. It might have been made of rare woods or bright brass, or bound in leather like a book.

But in the early 20th century, kaleidoscopes were either forgotten or ignored. Finally, in the 1970s, serious artists and craftspeople discovered that modern materials and methods made it possible to build scopes that created more exciting images than anything dreamed of.

Today many artisans are dedicated to experimenting with the kaleidoscope. They have discovered amazing new effects it can produce. These artists build kaleidoscopes that are true works of art.

There's a story behind every one of these scopes, and some of them are hard to believe. The tiniest scope we know of is like a little jewel. It's less than an inch long and weighs under an ounce. The biggest is a 6' x 12' monster—more than twice the size of a standard refrigerator—and weighs a quarter of a ton.

Nothing is too unusual to be used inside the object chamber of a modern scope. Some artists put in diamonds. Some insert ampules of colored liquid, seal the chamber and float objects in the liquid. You can get scopes with object chambers full of candy, or scopes with extra mirrors in the chamber itself, so you see a kaleidoscopic picture of your own eye.

The most exciting part of this kaleidoscope revival is that you're part of it now. The following chapters will show you new ways to join those who test the possibilities of their scopes and their imaginations.

The outsides may get as much attention as the insides. Cases can be made of wood, plastic or even gold. And the artists may shape them into forms you'd never expect—airplanes, fire-breathing dragons, pyramids, or magic wands.

Becoming a Scope Master

It's time to make the most of what you've learned about reflection, color and symmetry in your kaleidoscope. If you've completed most of the experiments and projects presented so far in this book, you're already on your way to becoming a scopemaster—someone who can find whole new ways to see the world.

A SCOPEMASTER'S KIT

Because a kaleidoscope's object chamber is usually small, the things that go inside it have to be small as well. You'll want a way to keep all those little things together.

Look for a sturdy storage box. A shoe box, tackle box, cigar box, or any other clean, strong container with a secure lid will work fine.

Begin a collection of things small enough to fit inside the object chamber. The most exciting objects to look at will probably be transparent or translucent; in a scope like the one in this kit, opaque objects will show up in silhouette.

IMPORTANT NOTE: It is possible to choke on small objects like the ones you're using. Never put anything from your object chamber collection in your mouth, and don't let anyone else do so either. A few sealable plastic bags in your scopemaster's box will help keep your collection safely organized.

Don't hesitate to put plenty of objects in the chamber at the same time. Up to a point, the more bits and pieces you put in the chamber the more intricate and exciting the picture will be.

But if you put in *too* many things, you may get a clog that blocks out the light. Always remember that reflected or refracted light reaching your eye is what makes the beautiful sights inside the scope. If the view is too dark, try shaking the scope gently or remove a few pieces so that the remaining pieces can move freely.

The list of ideas that follows should help you get your collection started. You'll want to try lots of other things, too. A big part of the fun of using your scope is thinking up new objects to put inside it.

TRANSLUCENTS AND TRANSPARENTS: You can find many different ways to add filtered color to your collection with objects such as these: Bingo chips, buttons, parts of old toys, marbles, colored cellophane or tissue paper, cut-up bits of plastic tubing or colored straws, tiny plastic Christmas tree lights, swizzle sticks, needle-point mesh, plastic toothpicks, barrettes, parts of old combs, broken bits of colored plastic, and discarded photographic slides or film negatives (color or black-and-white), cut down to fit inside the object case.

BUGS: Gently placing an ant, beetle, or even a firefly inside your scope will give you a very unusual, living picture! After a minute or two (*not longer*) of watching your insect actors, take them out and let them go free—they've earned it!

GLOW-IN-THE-DARK STICKERS: Hold them up to the light to "charge" them, then immediately put them in the object chamber. Keep the paper backing in place!

PLANTS: Try tiny flowers, petals, small pine cones and needles, leaves, vines, tendrils and seeds. Because symmetry is part of so many plants, they look especially interesting when their shapes are multiplied. They will not stay fresh for long in your scope, so don't forget to remove them after a short time.

TEXTURED SHAPES: Objects that show strong shape or texture, such as an airy feather or a few wisps pulled from a cotton puff, can create interesting silhouettes. Look for tiny gears and springs, or screws and hex nuts. Try popcorn, lace, cut-up bits of screening, seashells, gum-machine toys, neck chains, rubber bands, snaps or safety pins, uncooked pasta in elbow, alphabet, shell and wagon-wheel shapes.

MESSAGES: Words and pictures printed on paper thin enough to allow light to pass through will spill secret messages all over the inside of the scope. Try writing your message on clear bits of acetate using a permanent marker.

MINERALS: Look for clear or colored crystals, such as amethyst or rose quartz, that are small enough to fit in the object chamber (usually less than ½" across).

HOT!

Wow! Great!

Hello

COSTUME JEWELRY: Scour flea markets or garage sales in your neighborhood for old costume jewelry. It's often very cheap, and if you take the stones out of the settings, you'll get some real keepers for your kit.

A SCOPEMASTER'S MATERIALS

When you start to create your own scopes, you'll find that certain tools and materials will be needed for practically every project. Even if you are not about to start a scope project, keep a supply of these items just in case.

FLAT CARDBOARD: Posterboard, the smooth, stiff kind sold in sheets at art supply stores, is best for making mirrors. Rough, brown or gray cardboard is thinner and useful for other parts of the scope.

PAPER: Tracing paper in various thicknesses is always called for. Thin white paper, colored papers or specialty papers may create interesting effects in a scope.

DRAFTING TOOLS: An accurate ruler, a compass and even a protractor can be useful for creating new mirror systems for your scopes. If you're unsure how to use a compass or protractor, ask an adult for help.

PLASTIC: The most useful kind of plastic for scope projects is the kind used for takeout food. It's clear and stiff, but can be cut with scissors. Some toys and games are packed in this kind of plastic. Save it when you find it. Flexible plastic, such as acetate film, is used for making mirrors.

TUBES: Salt boxes, mailers, potato chip cans—any tube long enough and wide enough to accept mirrors can be a future scope. Keep your eyes open for these.

A Color-wheel Scope

One way to change the color of the view through the scope is to insert small pieces of the colored cellophane that come with the kit. For quick changes of color, make a color wheel.

YOU'LL NEED:

- ▲ Lightweight posterboard
- ▲ Clear cellophane tape
- ▲ One nail at least 2" long
- ▲ One soft-lead pencil
- ▲ Two rubber bands
- ▲ Scissors
- ▲ Tracing paper

1. Trace the shape on page 89 onto tracing paper with the pencil, then turn the tracing paper upside down and draw over the traced lines onto the posterboard.

2. Darken the marks on the posterboard if you need to and cut out the wheel. Tape the cellophane over the holes in the wheel.

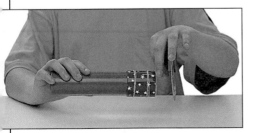

3. Poke the nail through the center of the wheel so it can turn, and use the rubber bands to fasten the nail to the side of your scope with the point in, as shown. Now you can spin the wheel and change the colors in your scope whenever you like.

More Wheels

YOU'LL NEED:

- ▲ Everything from previous project
- ▲ Colored pipe cleaners
- ▲ One new, unsharpened pencil or one chopstick
- ▲ One paper doily
- ▲ Clear plastic container lids
- ▲ Colored yarn
- ▲ Fishing line
- ▲ Beads
- ▲ Thumb tacks and pushpins
- ▲ Slip-on pencil erasers
- ▲ Plastic drinking straw

You can make many other wheels for unusual moving effects. The pictures that follow show simple wheels fastened to a pencil, chopstick, or dowel.

▲ Four colored pipe cleaners bundled together, with one more to wrap the bundle tightly around the end of a pencil. Remove the scope's object chamber and fasten the pencil to the scope with two rubber bands.

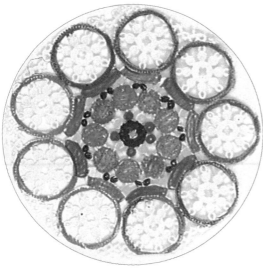

▲ Wheels made of clear or translucent plastic lids from margarine tubs, etc. These have small holes punched through with the nail, then are woven with pipe cleaners or yarn; threaded with beads and fishing line; drawn on with colored markers; glued with objects; taped together to trap objects in between.

▲ A small paper doily wheel. Color the doily or leave it white for a snowflake effect.

▲ Use the nail to punch the center hole in the lid, then fasten the lid to the eraser end of the pencil with a thumb tack or pushpin. If the lid hole is slightly larger than the tack or whatever holds it on, it will spin freely.

Double-wheel scopes provide great effects. You can make them in at least two ways.

▲ For a quick, temporary double wheel, you'll need two pushpins and a slip-on eraser. Assemble as shown. Spin the wheels slowly, in opposite directions. Always put the most transparent wheel closest to the scope.

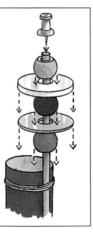

▲ For a more permanent way, find "spacers"—large beads, tube pasta, hex nuts, etc; an unsharpened pencil or dowel; a pushpin. Make the holes in the disks large enough to slip over the dowel or pencil. Assemble as shown.

Attach a store-bought or homemade pinwheel, then spin it by blowing at it through a drinking straw while you hold the scope to your eye.

▲ **Remove the pinwheel from its original stick. Use a #4 plastic knitting needle or a dowel that fits through the center hole. Slip on a spacer to either side of the wheel. (If using a dowel, add a pushpin or thumbtack at the end.) Attach to the tube as before.**

▲ **To make a wheel for any other size scope, measure the diameter (the widest distance across the end of the tube) of the scope, and double that number to get the diameter of the wheel.**

P R O J E C T

Scribble Scope

Use white paper—the thinner it is, the more light will pass through. Tracing paper works well, but you can use almost any kind of paper as long as it's not too thick.

Turn your imagination loose—you won't know how a drawing will look inside the scope until you try it. Simple colored shapes are transformed when you see them in the scope.

YOU'LL NEED:

- ▲ *Tracing paper or thin white paper*
- ▲ *Colored markers*
- ▲ *Scissors*
- ▲ *Sharpened pencil*

1. Take the clear plastic disk out of your object chamber and trace a page of circles onto your paper, then put the disk back in the scope.

2. Using colored markers, draw pictures inside each of the circles on the paper. Fill as much of the circle with color as you can. Cut out the circles and fit one into the end cap. If necessary, trim the circle a bit to make it lie flat.

PROJECT

Holy Teleido

You've already discovered what a teleidoscope does. This simple scope without an object case gives you a chance to see the whole world in kaleidoscopic patterns (see page 24).

Begin using it by looking at the faces you like best—your friends and the people you live with. Then scout your house. Check out the bathroom mirror, a fish tank, a fireplace, a Christmas tree. Even wiggling your fingers in front of the scope makes interesting designs.

If you have a lazy Susan—a revolving tray—try loading it up with flowers, toys and other objects that look interesting but would be too big to fit inside the object chamber. Turn the tray and see what happens.

To really see what this scope can do, take a teleidoscope walk. (Don't look through the scope while you're moving, or it may be a very *short* stroll!) One of the best things about this scope is that you'll see kaleidoscopic movement everywhere. Look around your neighborhood, at nearby parks and stores, and especially at things that move on their own—cars, animals, kids on bikes and swings.

A 1¾" Lucite ball fitted into the end of the open object chamber will transform the interesting views from your teleidoscope into unforgettable scenes. The ball acts as a lens, creating a wall of sharply focused images.

*T**he curved surface of the Lucite ball will curve the image and reduce it in size.*

PROJECT

Chip Scope

Here's an easy scope you can make using a potato chip tube. These instructions show you one good way to make mirrors, but you can use any of the other methods you learn in the book.

YOU'LL NEED:

- Tall, slender can, the kind that comes with potato chips stacked inside
- 1½" x 1½" square of acetate or other clear plastic
- Three 8½" x 2⅜" pieces of clear acetate, or drafting film
- Three 8½" x 2⅜" pieces of black construction paper
- Three 8½" x 2⅜" pieces of cardboard
- 2⅞" circle of acetate or other clear plastic
- 9" x ⅝" strip of cardboard
- Hammer and nail
- Small, pointed scissors
- Rubber cement and white glue

1. Clean the crumbs and grease from the tube and lid. Use the hammer and nail to punch an eyehole in the center of the metal end of the can. Holding the scissors closed, push it into the hole and turn it around until you've widened the hole to about ½" across. When the hole is big enough, tip the scissors as shown to press down the rough edges inside the can.

2. Clean the square of plastic to remove dirt or fingerprints and drop it into the can. This piece protects your eye. Remember, every scope you make should have an eye guard like this.

3. Slide two strips of cardboard into the tube, making the same "V" you used when you put together your kit scope (see page 8), then slip the third strip of cardboard across the top to form a triangle. The three strips of black paper go in next, *inside the triangle,* and then the three strips of plastic.

4. Look through the eyehole to make sure the mirror parts form a neat equilateral (equal-sided) triangle. If they're not placed just right, adjust them. (The reflections from these mirrors will not be quite as sharp as those from the mirrors in your kit scope.)

5. Now put the 2⅞" plastic circle on top of the mirrors. Glue the circle in place, using white glue, around the edges of the circle. (See p. 69 for picture.)

6. Rub the flat, wide side of the 9" x ⅝" strip of cardboard over the edge of a table to "soften" it enough to curl smoothly around the inside of your tube.

Apply some rubber cement to the outside of the curled cardboard and on the inside of the tube in the space between the clear plastic circle and the end of the can. Let the cement dry on both surfaces, then press the cardboard ring into place, snug against the clear circle. It will hold the circle down and close any gaps between the circle and the tube.

7. Now put whatever objects you want into the chamber you've formed, and use the can's plastic lid to close them in. The lid is translucent and frosted, fits snugly, and can be taken off and replaced again and again without damaging the tube, so it makes a perfect end cap. Because this scope has the chamber built into the tube, you'll have to turn the whole tube when you look through it.

Decorate the outside of the tube with wrapping paper.

MAKING AN END CAP

— — —

To make a cap for any size tube, trace a disk the diameter of the tube end onto clear, stiff plastic and cut it out. Scuff it with sandpaper for a "frosted" look. Lay the disk on top of the tube end. Wrap tape (at least ¾" wide) around the top edge of the tube so that ¼" sticks up above the rim. Snip the tape evenly all around (snips should be about ¼" apart). Now, one at a time, fold the tabs over onto the disk (tabs will overlap).

DISK

TAPE

Squishy Scopes

YOU'LL NEED:

- Plastic jar with screw lid
- Masking tape
- Water
- Household wire
- White ribbon, 1" wide
- Food coloring
- Salad oil
- Dishwashing soap
- Glycerin or corn syrup

Ever open your eyes under water? Things look different—they float and drift in a graceful way that you don't usually see above the surface. You can make a fluid-chamber scope that will create these magical floating views. You'll want an adult's help when making it because it can be messy.

To begin, you'll need a jar with a screw lid. Vitamin jars are ideal; other possibilities are clear plastic spice or medicine jars or other small, round, clear plastic containers. The jar must fit *tightly* into the object case of your scope with the end cap removed. If necessary, you can wrap masking tape around the bottom of the jar to make it fit snugly into the object chamber. The jar will extend beyond the end of the scope. Put some

▲ Add a drop or two of food coloring to the water. Notice that this works like your filters in changing the colors of objects in the jar.

▲ Put a little dish soap into the jar with water and shake it, *hard*.

▲ Try filling the jar with glycerin, which is clear but nearly as thick as pancake syrup. You can buy it at any drugstore. Things you put into it will sort of ooze around as you turn the scope. (It's possible to use corn syrup, but it gets sticky.)

▲ Pour in a little salad oil. Because it's lighter than water and doesn't mix with it, the oil may separate into blobs. You can put food coloring in this one, too. It will stain only the water, not the oil. Your view may look like the ocean.

waterproof objects from your collection into the jar, then fill it with water. *Tighten the jar lid.* Fit the clear end of the jar into the object chamber and have a look. If your plastic jar is too long or too narrow to fit into the object chamber, you can construct another kind of holder with household wire or ribbons and rubber bands.

▲ For a temporary attachment, wrap a piece of 1"-wide, white ribbon over the jar and secure it with several twists of a rubber band. To make this version permanent, glue the ribbon and substitute more ribbon, glued down, for the rubber band. Let the glue dry thoroughly.

▲ Remove the turning end of the scope. Cut a 22"-long piece of flexible household wire and wrap it around the end of the tube and the jar, as shown. Tape will hold the wire in place.

PROJECT

Flashlight Scope

A plastic flashlight without batteries makes a good housing for a simple kaleidoscope. For as little as a dollar, you can buy the makings of a sturdy little scope that comes with the object chamber built right in. You will need some adult help with this project.

YOU'LL NEED:

▲ *Inexpensive plastic flashlight*
▲ *¾" square of clear plastic*
▲ *Cellophane or masking tape*
▲ *Clear plastic circle*
▲ *White glue*
▲ *Sandpaper*

1. Start by unscrewing the light bulb end; take out the bulb assembly and the spring that holds the batteries in place. Ask an adult to drill a ⅜" hole in the center of the other end of the flashlight. Drop in the small plastic square eye guard.

2. Trace the narrow end of the flashlight and determine the size of the mirrors. (See page 72, Further Reflection, to learn how to do this.) You'll create your mirrors using any of the materials and methods shown on pages 70–75.

To determine the mirror length, measure the flashlight from end to end and subtract 1½" from that length.

3. Tape the mirrors together in a triangular shape (see page 74) and slide them into the tube.

4. Cut a clear plastic circle to fit into the tube on top of the mirrors. Use a few blobs of white glue around the edges to hold it in place. Put the scope aside until the glue is completely dry.

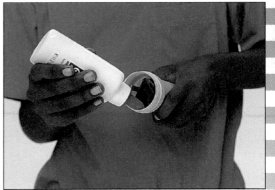

5. Then put whatever objects you like into the end of the flashlight tube and screw the end cap back on. The clear plastic lens of the flashlight has become the outer disk of your object chamber. If you prefer a "frosted," translucent disk, scuff that outer disk with sandpaper.

PROJECT

Other Mirrors

It's possible to make kaleidoscopes even with home-made mirrors. If you made a Chip Scope, you've already seen that simple pieces of clear acetate with black paper backing can make effective mirrors.

Here's another way to create your own mirrors using

YOU'LL NEED:

▲ Acetate film or sheet .01mm thick
▲ Black or white posterboard
▲ Sharp scissors
▲ Spray adhesive

Here are some other reflective surfaces that will work: mirrored Plexiglas; clear or black Plexiglas, 1/16"–1/8" thick; black vinyl.

acetate film or sheet, available at art supply stores or print shops. Buy a big sheet, 25" x 30"—this will make lots of mirrors. You will need an adult's help with this work.

1. Cut a large piece of posterboard to a manageable size—for example, 12" x 12". Then cut the acetate film so that it's about ½" larger all around than the posterboard.

2. *FOLLOW ALL SAFETY PRECAUTIONS ON THE CAN OF SPRAY ADHESIVE.* **Find a large work area with plenty of fresh air coming through it. Lay newspaper on the table or floor under and around the posterboard. Have an adult lightly spray the top side of the posterboard, making sure the spray covers all four outside edges.**

3. Lay the acetate or film on the posterboard so all four edges overlap. Rub the acetate or film flat with your hand. Make sure any air bubbles are flattened out by rubbing from the center to the outside edge of the posterboard.

4. Trim off the overlapping film. Now you are ready to cut the large mirror sheet to whatever sizes you need. You can mark your cutting lines on the back side of the sheet.

PROJECT

Further Reflection

YOU'LL NEED:

▲ **Tracing paper**

▲ **Ruler**

▲ **Compass**

▲ **Black posterboard**

▲ **Cellophane or masking tape**

An easy way to make a big change in the view inside your kaleidoscope is to make a two-mirror system by substituting a dark panel for one of the mirrors. Just slip one mirror out of the scope, trace it on thin, dark cardboard, cut out the rectangle and slide it into the scope.

Instead of the three-mirror pattern—triangles filling the whole view—you'll see a centered, six-part figure that may remind you of a pie cut in pieces. As always, you're seeing one "slice" that represents the real objects in the chamber, two more that are first-generation reflections of the original, and others that are reflections of reflections.

The three angles of a triangle must add up to 180 degrees: Substituting one cardboard strip for one of your kit mirrors gives you the same 60-degree angle as the three-mirror system, where all angles are equal (60+60+60=180).

You can create even more complex patterns with a two-mirror system by changing the angle between the two mirrors.

1. To construct a narrow-angle system for two mirrors, trace the outline of your scope's tube end on a piece of tracing paper. Use a ruler to draw a center line across the circle at its widest point. Then use the compass to draw another, ⅛" smaller circle inside it. This equals the thickness of the tube walls.

2. Place the tracing over one of the angles on the angle guide on page 75 so that the point of the angle touches the inside edge of the inner circle and the center line lies on top of the dotted line. If necessary, use a ruler to extend the angle lines until they touch the far side of the inner circle. Measure one of the lines to determine the width of the mirrors.

3. Now draw a line connecting the two lines. That third line will be the width of the cardboard strip. The length will be the same as the two mirrors.

4. Once you know the correct width, figuring out the mirror length is easy: It should be at least two-and-one-half times the width. If your mirrors are 2" wide, for example, they should be at least 5" long. The mirrors can be longer if you like; just be sure they're short enough to fit inside the tube and leave enough space for an object chamber.

5. Lay the pieces side by side on a piece of paper, shiny sides down, and join them with tape, as shown.

6. Then lift the taped pieces and make a triangular tube of them, shiny sides to the inside. Tape the last two edges together, then run a strip of tape all the way around the outside. Slide the mirror assembly into the tube. If it doesn't fit snugly, remove it and wrap it with paper towels or felt.

The pictures on the next page show what you can expect to see from two-mirror systems with different angles.

▲ To make a four-mirror system, use the 90-degree angle guide, as in Step 2. If you place the point of the angle so that two opposite sides are longer, your view will be more interesting.

90°

ANGLE GUIDE

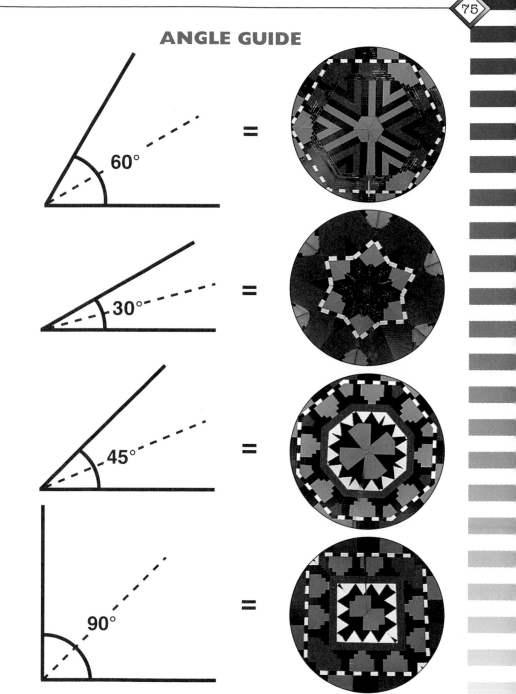

PROJECT

Shadow Scopes

Changing the light in your scope will give you new views to see. You can use the shadow method with or without objects in the object chamber. When you turn the chamber, anything inside will fall across the light beams passing through—and will appear and vanish again within the kaleidoscopic image. Tape colored cellophane to one side of the disk for a different effect.

▲ Using the end of your scope tube, trace a cardboard disk. Cut out the disk and cut or punch holes of different shapes into it. Make plenty of holes and cutout shapes—you'll only be able to see objects where light can enter to outline them. Fit it into the bottom of the end cap, and put the cap back on the scope.

A Mirrored Tunnel

For a very simple mirror switch using your kit scope, cut a 5½" x 6½" piece of clear flexible plastic or silver Mylar. Remove the object chamber and take out the mirror assembly. Roll up the plastic or Mylar and fit it inside. There's no need to fasten it—just let it spread out to line the inside of the scope. Then put the object chamber back on.

This mirror will treat you to a spiraling image that's quite different than the flat-mirror kinds you're used to seeing. It works best when you put lots of brightly colored objects in the case and flood it with light.

Polarizing Scopes

You've read about polarizing filters earlier in the book. If you get a pair of filters (try one of the sources in the list on page 88), or can salvage a set from an old pair of sunglasses, fit one into the eyepiece of your kit scope and one into the cap of the object chamber.

1. Using the two clear disks from your scope, trace two circles on your polarized plastic and cut them out.

When you turn the object chamber, you'll see the view grow darker and lighter, just as it did when you were experimenting with the filters before. But the change in light levels is even more striking when it's combined with the kaleidoscopic image of things in the object chamber.

For a really different polarizing effect, you'll need a little bit of plastic—for instance, the clear wrapper from a gumball or a caramel or other piece of candy. You can also

2. Remove the mirror assembly from the scope. Remove the protective covering, if any, from the disks, and slip the larger one into the end cap and the smaller one in the eyepiece end of the scope.Replace the mirrors in the scope.

use clear soda straws, crumpled-up lengths of clear tape (try to fold the sticky part inside), or even pieces of clean, clear plastic cut from take-out food containers, with a few pieces of clear tape attached. Tuck the pieces inside the object chamber.

You should see a spectrum of color in almost every piece of plastic. Turn the object chamber and watch the colors change.

PROJECT

Rocket Scope

YOU'LL NEED:

▲ **Colored plastic Easter eggs, the kind that separate into two halves**

▲ **Wide colored tape**

▲ **Tracing paper**

▲ **Colored cardboard or posterboard**

A little extra decoration can make your scope look like something completely new—in this case, a rocket. The basic body of the scope is a two- or three-mirror system inside a tube.

1. Add objects to the object chamber. Then fasten the egg to the end of the scope with colored tape.

Use the same methods for making mirrors described on pages 70–71. To create the nose cone, use the pointy half of a colored plastic Easter egg. Look for a light-colored plastic, to allow the most light into the scope.

2. Trace the fin design shown on page 89 onto tracing paper; flip it over and retrace onto colored posterboard; cut out three or four of them. Fold along the dotted line, and glue the folded flap to the eyehole end of the scope tube as shown in the picture. (Don't let the fins extend beyond the end of the tube.)

Add space-related art, such as stickers in the shape of stars, the moon or planets, to the tube and start your countdown.

PROJECT

Teleido-snap!

You can easily shoot good kaleidoscopic photo-graphs if you have a camera that can focus to within one foot.

1. Make a piece of acetate-on-board mirror that measures 12" x 12" (see page 70). On the back side of the mirror, measure and mark a point 6" from two opposite edges to find the center line. Then measure and mark the two edges as shown, dividing the edges into segments of 5", 2" and 5" along one side, and 2", 5" and 2" along the opposite side. Now draw connecting lines and cut along those lines. You'll end up with three tapered mirrors, each one 2" wide at one end and 5" wide at the other.

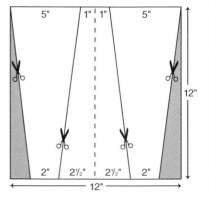

Diagram labels: 5" | 1" | 1" | 5" (top); 12" (right side); 2" | 2½" | 2½" | 2" (bottom); 12" (bottom)

2. Use large rubber bands to assemble the mirrors into a triangular tube, with the shiny sides in and all the wide ends together.

To take your pictures, just aim the *small* end of the assembly (which its inventor, Ann Franklin, calls a Teleidosnap) at the subject you want to photograph. Set the camera focus for one foot, then hold the camera at the big end of the assembly and snap your picture. That's all it takes.

DECORATION IDEAS

To decorate your scopes or scopemaster kit, you can use some of the ideas on pages 38 and 42. Of course, there's no rule that your decorations have to be symmetrical.

Cover the tube with glitter. Wrap it in yarn or ribbon. Glue on fabric or wallpaper. Use the craft-shop material called Friendly Plastic to create shapes you can stick on the scope. Glue old magazine art, comics or photographs around the tube. Choose a theme, such as sports, nature, astronomy or geography, and search old magazines for related pictures you can paste to the tube. Then coat the tube with diluted white paste or clear acrylic, which you can buy in an art store.

Create a design using small pieces of paper, beans or macaroni. Or you may want to try building up the body of the scope with papier mâché—turn it into a fish, a dragon or a troll.

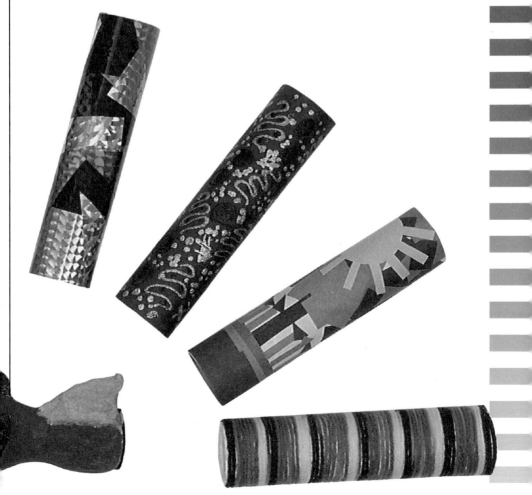

HOLDERS AND STANDS

You may want to give your best scope a display stand, just like an old-fashioned parlor scope. Scope stands show off beautiful scopes, but they can also serve to angle the scope more precisely, so you can share a special view with others.

▲ A clamp holder made from hardware store supplies is a great way to support a through-the-window scope.

▲ If you lose one knit glove, put the other to good use! Stuff it *tightly* with paper, then use a needle and thread to gather all the fingers together, starting at the pinky. Take one more stitch to connect the pointer finger to the thumb. Fasten the glove to a piece of plywood with a row of push-pins or thumb-tacks.

▲ This stand is made out of a shoebox,
the plastic cap from a soda bottle, a ¾"-wide wooden stick, and a
paper-towel tube. Glue the bottle cap to the inside center of the
box lid. Cut the cardboard tube from a paper towel roll to about
one-half the length of the scope. Slice the
tube in half lengthwise, and glue it firmly to
one end of the stick. Assemble the stand
by inserting the wooden stick through a
hole in the center of the box bottom and
resting it in the bottle cap.
Decorate and add scope.

SOURCES

SCIENCE AND ART SUPPLIERS

Listed here are suppliers of specialized materials you may want for your kaleidoscopes. Free catalogs are available from all of them.

AMERICAN SCIENCE & SURPLUS
601 LINDEN PLACE
EVANSTON, IL 60202
(708) 475-8440

All sorts of surplus odds and ends for experiments. You never know what they have. The catalog is lots of fun.

EDMUND SCIENTIFIC
101 EAST GLOUCESTER PIKE
BARRINGTON, NJ 08007-1380
(609) 547-3488

All sorts of science supplies, including polarizing filters; lenses; and optical supplies.

AIN PLASTIC
PO BOX 7655
LANCASTER, PA 17604-7655
(800) 345-5440

Plastic supplies, including Lucite, and acrylic balls; sheet; and tubing.

WARNER CRIVELLARO
1855 WEAVERSVILLE RD.
ALLENTOWN, PA 18103
(800) 523-4242

Supplies for stained-glass artists (which can be useful for kaleidoscope artists); first-surface mirrors.

FRANKLIN ART GLASS
222 EAST SYCAMORE ST.
COLUMBUS, OH 43206
(800) 848-7683

Supplies for stained-glass artists, first-surface mirrors; stained-glass kaleidoscope kits.

UNITED ART GLASS
1032 EAST OGDEN
SUITE 128
NAPERVILLE, IL 60563
(800) 323-9760

Supplies for stained-glass artists.

GENERAL SUPPLIERS

For most of your kaleidoscope needs, these stores are really the best bet and the most fun. You might find tubes you never could have imagined at a discount or variety store, or unusual viewable objects at a stationery or office-supply store

HARDWARE STORES

SUPERMARKETS

DISCOUNT STORES

CRAFT SUPPLY STORES

FABRIC AND SEWING SUPPLY STORES

KNITTING AND NEEDLEWORK STORES

ART SUPPLY AND FRAMING STORES

GLAZING SUPPLY AND REPAIR STORES

BEAD STORES

PHOTOGRAPHIC SUPPLY STORES

SHAPES TO TRACE

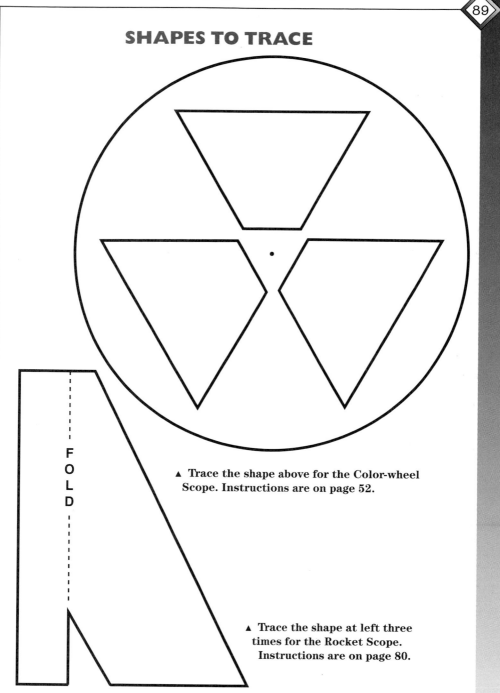

F O L D

▲ Trace the shape above for the Color-wheel
Scope. Instructions are on page 52.

▲ Trace the shape at left three
times for the Rocket Scope.
Instructions are on page 80.